Saratoga Ca.
May 24 - 1991

To Sensei Miss Gark's
6th grade
Rolling Hill School.

今 エ
う ム
も ス

山本

889R.

JAMES IMAHARA
SON OF IMMIGRANTS

By James M. Imahara
as told to Anne Butler Poindexter

ACKNOWLEDGEMENTS

I gratefully acknowledge the assistance and support of my wife and all my children, especially May and Walter who provided emotional and financial support, and Lily who did all the legwork and suffered through our many lengthy interview sessions.

Namua-Mida-Butu-
Gassho

FOREWORD

Writing a Sociology term paper while attending L.S.U. in Baton Rouge, La., during recent years, 1973-79, I became aware, for the first time as an adult, of the plight of the Japanese-Americans in the United States. Astonished and dismayed at a history untold, a minority group caught in a political and economic struggle beyond their comprehension, I felt, as the daughter of a Nisei, that the story should be told by those of us who had lived through it.

This hope for a book was only a dream I kept to myself until I met Anne Poindexter, Director of the Council on Aging in West Feliciana, who hired me as a bookkeeper. Later I found out that she was a writer and journalist, and approached her about helping "Pop" write a book.

Overwhelmed, I asked Pop if he would be willing to write a memoir. His reply was that for several years on his periodic trips to Hot Wells near Alexandria, La., he had been recording his story in Japanese, wondering who would help him translate it into English. Pop's desire was to record the story of his life so that his children and grandchildren would know what life had been like for the Japanese-Americans in the beginning and how the Japanese spirit overcame all obstacles. Then, there was my brother Walter, the financier, who was also secretly hoping for a story about Pop and his family.

A dream, a hope, a thanksgiving, a story of one man's journey through life, his thoughts, emotions, philosophy, as a young lad, a family man, a responsible and caring person who shared the burden of his people—the Issei.

However, *James Imahara—Son of Immigrants* also tells the story of a Japanese-American community; what happened to him and his family was a common experience for nearly all. The helplessness of social racism and discrimination, the outrage of political maneuvers, became dim shadows as spirits rose, personal victories were won and shattered lives were replaced by grander dreams. As I have been told, it is not what happens to us that matters, but how we come out of it.

Lily Imahara Metz

iii

DEDICATION

To my ancestors

my father Minezo,
my mother Mika—
also to my father-in-law
Sasaichi Sunada
and mother-in-law Shikiyo.

KI-O

The cover illustration, executed with brush and ink by James Imahara for reproduction, is the Japanese character for Ki-O, "happy old man," his haiku pen name, which he uses now in his Plum stage of life.

Like the pages of a book, the days of a man's life fall into distinct and separate chapters. To the Japanese way of thinking, there are three major stages of life:

PINE (Sho-Matsu)
BAMBOO (Chiku-Take)
PLUM (Bai-Ume)

The Pine stage is the early life, up to age 25, a happy time for James Imahara, encompassing carefree childhood, school days, rural life, membership in community organizations, marriage and the birth of children in the pre-war days.

The Bamboo stage was a 40-year-long period of struggle, up to age 65. These were the years of starting an agricultural enterprise, the outbreak of World War II, a dark and uncertain age of evacuation, internment, resettlement in Louisiana, building up the nursery business and educating the children.

The Plum stage, the final years, encompasses the later post-war years of retirement and the enjoyment of hobbies such as wood carving and the creation of haikus; during this period came the honor of the decoration by the government of Japan and the joy of the trip to that country.

PATENT OF DECORATION

The fifth class of the Order of The Sacred Treasure is hereby conferred upon

Mr. James Imahara,
American Citizen,
by His Majesty, the Emperor of Japan
20th of the 12th month of 52nd year
of Showa (1977)

Takeo Fukuda,
Prime Minister

Minezo Imahara
born Hiroshima
came to U.S. late 1800s
   about 1895
died 1941

Mika Nishita
born Hiroshima
came to U.S. in 1900 as
   picture bride, selected by
   groom's relative in Japan
died 1940

James Masaru Imahara
born Watsonville California
   Sept. 4, 1903

married June 26, 1927 in Sacramento California to

Haruka Sunada
born Sacramento, California
Jan. 19, 1909

their children:
1. Satsuki (May) born Sacramento
2. Chizuko (Helen) born Sacramento; deceased
3. Mayumi (Flora) born Sacramento
4. Miyuki (Jane) born Sacramento
5. Yuriko (Lily) born Sacramento
6. Manabu (Walter) born Sacramento
7. Kay (John) born Sacramento
8. Etsuko (Irene) born Sacramento
9. Jun born Fresno Assembly Center
10. Philip born New Orleans

The last two children were given no Japanese name due to war.

The soft pink flush of a cherry blossom—the hard quick flash of a Samurai sword. An appreciation of nature and an artistic view of the world, the love of creative arts, a striving for perfection and an emphasis on mannerliness, the importance of adhering to the straight and narrow path, a living and a dying by a rigid code of courage and honor, a life of hard work and determination, a respect for the land and a passion for growing things, a desire for constant improvement and a thirst for education—these elements of the Japanese character contributed to the dream of golden opportunity which inspired the Japanese immigrations to the United States of America a century ago, in the late 1800's.

Japan was a small country with a large population. The economy was in a decline after several centuries of isolation. Emigration had been banned for centuries. Then a new emperor opened up trade, which had been held in disrespect in this Samurai culture. With trade and exposure to foreign ways came the American dream of roads paved with riches.

Succumbing to the lure of golden opportunities and financial new horizons, the immigrants arrived in this country after 1890 with little in the way of material possessions. They had to overcome almost insurmountable odds to succeed on the West Coast, where most settled, but succeed they did, especially in the field of agriculture, where they made spectacular contributions.

By the time most Japanese arrived, the Chinese Exclusion Acts first passed in 1882 had set the tone for Oriental exclusion on the West Coast. Fleeing poverty and oppression in China, these earlier immigrants had arrived by the thousands in the mid-19th century to work the gold fields, build the railroads with cheap labor, and begin significant irrigation and land reclamation projects. Misunderstood, hated and feared by white workers, the Chinese were prohibited from becoming naturalized citizens and their treatment set the tone for the reception of the Japanese immigrants later in that century. Even the first Japanese arrivals were already stigmatized, with only the lowest employment open to them upon arrival.

Mika Nishita Imahara, mother of James, arrived in the United States around 1900 as a picture bride.

Minezo Imahara, father of James, immigrated from Hiroshima as a young man.

Into this picture came Minezo Imahara, born to a Hiroshima family with proud Samurai ancestors. He arrived in this country around 1895, having come a roundabout way, first to Hawaii, then to Guatemala, then to San Francisco, and finally to Watsonville, California, a farming community on Monterey Bay. Imahara arrived seeking new horizons, golden opportunities. Like two of his brothers, he was lured by the American dream.

The dream didn't last long. He faced constant struggle, laboring from sunup to sundown for a dollar a day. Like a large percentage of other Japanese immigrants of this time, Imahara would have gone home had he been able to save the money for transportation, but he couldn't.

Wise relatives in Japan decided to settle the immigrant down

James Imahara, age 4

by sending a picture bride, Mika Nishita, also born in Hiroshima. She arrived in the United States around 1900, going straight to Watsonville. With her arrival, the Imahara roots were set a little deeper in American soil, especially after the arrival of four children, James Masaru Imahara, May Kimiko Imahara, David Hiromu Imahara, and Henry Masao Imahara.

James Imahara, known as Jimmy in childhood, that's me, the American son of immigrants. This is my story.

I have kept this thing in my chest for half a century. Today I'm going to tell you. What I say is honest. It is the truth. It is the story of the Japanese-American in this country.

I did not have a glorious or colorful childhood. My father and mother were immigrants. We had a modest life, yet we did not go hungry. We were not the poorest, but we had no modern conveniences.

Yet we were happy, probably much more so then than now.

Son of the immigrant, that's the way I title myself. I was happiest in childhood and early life, from birth to early teens. In the Japanese way of thinking, we are born with no sin, pure and innocent. From 20 on to 40 or 50, life is hard, dark, filled with sin. It reverses again in later age, back to goodness, so we can die in peace. My early life was happy; from about age 20 through the evacuation, war and relocation, it was all struggle, dark times. Now I am happy again in my old age.

Japanese Association, Watsonville, Calif., 1900. Minezo Imahara on first row, extreme left.

Home of James Redmond, Watsonville, Calif.

In Watsonville, where I was born, my father was a truck farmer who sold crops. The Alien Land Act prohibited him and other Japanese immigrants from owning land. Before he started truck farming, he worked for a big apple and beet farmer for $1 a day. Jim Redmond was the big farmer; he and his sister gave their names and served as godparents to me and my sister May.

Jim Redmond was an influential person. My father subcontracted for sugar beets, and had an orchard. But Japanese don't like to work for anyone; we're independent, all Japanese feel that way. After my father went to farming, he didn't make anything, but he was his own boss.

Mr. Redmond said, "Jimmy is like a little gopher," when he found apples with little teeth marks on them. Gophers were the real enemy of California farmers in those days. My father was asked to trap them. In the morning he set out flagged traps, which he collected in the evening. He'd cut the tails off, and Jim Redmond paid him 5¢ a tail. That was big money in those days. He'd put the tails in a Bull Durham sack with a drawstring.

In 1905, when I was two years old, the San Francisco earthquake hit. Watsonville was maybe 100 miles south. We felt the big tremor. My mother later recalled that when the quake came, she wanted me outside, but I was so scared I went in the house and hid under the bed.

My father was very artistic. He made a stove, a *kudo*, out of straw and soil and lime, an open fire with three holes over it. Rice tastes so different when cooked on a strong wood fire. We ate the most delicious things. Mama made thick pancakes, and grape and strawberry jelly.

Our bathtub was outside, 4' × 4' boards, three feet deep. We would heat water over the fire, then put it in the tub. We had to hand pump it from the well. According to the traditional Japanese way of bathing, you wash outside, then jump into the tub with water clear up to your chin. Children had to be held in the tub.

James and May Imahara at 4 years and 1½ years

The bathhouse was separate from the house. The *kudo* was outside too, and we often ate by it. I like it that way, old style. I carried the children to the tub; we'd soap up and wash outside, jump into the tub, warm up, then off to bed. Now they pipe in hot water, but in my day tubs had metal bottoms with fire underneath to heat up.

I went to a little red one-room school in Watsonville, the public school on Beach Road, with one teacher for a dozen students from grades one through eight. There I learned English, since my parents spoke mostly Japanese. Mrs. White, the teacher, taught the 3 Rs and beautiful writing. We learned songs like "Pussy in the Well." I was very timid; the first day my father took me to school, but I ran home at recess.

We lived in the country. The school was five miles or more away. There was no road, just a cow path or buggy trail. I rode to school every day on a second-hand bicycle.

Transportation in those days was by horse and buggy or wagon. There were no automobiles; there was no electricity. I remember I used to get to clean the chimneys of our oil lamps since my hand was the smallest. I did other chores too, like feeding chickens, but not farming. My father had a team of horses, a buckboard, a plow, nothing much more.

On Sundays and holidays, we went clam hunting with the family and neighbors at the Watsonville beach about five miles away. Clams were so plentiful you could rake them up with your feet. We'd have a clam bake, and fish for sea bass. This is the kind of fun we had. Watsonville was apple country, so there was an annual apple show and a state fair with amusements, big tents, parades.

There were a few other Japanese families in the area, about a dozen. I recall no feeling of discrimination as a child; that came later, in my teens. The Japanese children went to Japanese school; later, in Sacramento, there would be a harmonious international school.

My father was born about 150 years ago, in Hiroshima. He was in his 40's when he left Japan. Everything there was a failure, and he came to start a new life in the United States. He had no formal schooling.

1918, Japanese School, above

1916, Lincoln Public School, Sacramento, below

He had difficulty reading and writing. But he was a man with a firm constitution, who brought up his family in the Spartan way, strict discipline with softness. He had great love for his children. He had come from a feudal age in Japan, the land of the sword and the Samurai, but he was a man of firm, gentle character who was soft spoken and who had no trouble with anybody.

His three sons and daughter were raised in a strict way with discipline, but he never laid a hand on his children, never raised his voice. He was a fine person.

My mother was firm too, yet kind and gentle. She would comfort when Papa would scold. If one is strict, one must also be gentle. She taught me arithmetic, over and over; it is still in me, just like a song. The first time I left home, to go to the school dormitory when I was 13 or 14, she reminded me to wash behind my ears when I washed my face, and showed me how to unwrinkle shirts. She warned me not to stand outside store windows looking or to lay a hand on other people's property. Her teachings have stayed with me all my life.

They made a wonderful family. My mother had been 20 years younger when they married. Picture brides were not uncommon arrangements. Some of the prospective grooms lied about their ages; one bald man had to keep his hat on when greeting his bride.

In Watsonville, I went to school in the Buddhist church, as there was no real Japanese school to supplement public school. The minister's wife taught me my *Iro-ha* (ABC's) at the dining table in the parsonage; I mastered them and can read and write Japanese fluently still, in my 80s.

Before passage of the Alien Land Act in 1920, my family had moved to Sacramento. There was a sizable Japanese community in Sacramento. My father had a friend there. We moved from Watsonville, which was small and limited, to Sacramento, the capital city, in search of more opportunity. We had also lost our pea crop in Watsonville in a killing frost, so we went by train to stay with my father's friend for awhile.

From 1915 to 1916 I attended a Buddhist boarding school, the only Japanese school in Sacramento, which had about 50 to

70 students. After two years there, a small Japanese school opened in my neighborhood, which I attended. I went to public English school in the mornings and to Japanese school in the afternoons to learn the language, the 3 Rs, the history and traditions and geography of Japan. I wasn't vitally interested in it then, and have forgotten most of it.

At this time I could feel the discrimination against the Japanese, well before the war years. Nobody knows why Japan attacked, but I know it takes two to tango. The historical root of the attack is not known; we only know the ugliness of the attack. We need to know both sides.

Sierra School in Sacramento, 1920. James Imahara, 17, third from right, third row.

In Sacramento, my father began an independent strawberry farm, and went into grape production, too. Strawberries were easier, with a faster turnover. Grapes take longer to get the first crop. We just barely made a living; strawberries sold cheaply then, and the price didn't rise until the war years.

My father was not a young man. He was 20 years older than my mother. As the first born, I helped him after school, so my education was necessarily limited. I did not even get to finish high school; I had only 7 years of school, but jumped ahead and was able to finish all eight years of grammar school in those seven years. After that I was self taught; I studied at night.

Imahara family portrait. From left, Henry, Minezo, James, David, Mika, May.

When I was 20, I purchased 60 acres of farmland. My father, a Japanese, was prohibited from owning land due to the Alien Land Act, but I was an American citizen. Some Japanese formed corporations to get around the prohibition against ownership of land. In 1919, for example, I was secretary and charter member of the Florin Buddhist Church. We formed a corporation to buy land for the church. I was only 16 years old, but since I was an American citizen and could purchase land, my name is on that deed. I was married in that church, and my parents' funeral services were held there.

Imahara home in Sacramento, Calif.

On my own 60 acres I raised strawberries, grapes, and an orchard of fruit trees. By a few years before the war, I was also raising poultry for meat and egg production.

I had a two-story house, above average for that time and place among the Japanese community. My grape orchard came right to the porch, and I was taking up to 200 chickens to market every week.

Front entrance to Imahara home and property, Sacramento, 1930

This was a busy period of my life. I was bilingual and about the oldest *Nisei,* so I helped the Japanese immigrants who couldn't speak or write English, the first generation immigrants called *Issei.* They needed help to resettle; they didn't know how to buy a horse or a plow, or how to lease land. There was a three-year limit on leases; at the end of three years, Japanese had to re-lease or move.

I was a real good busybody; farming on my own, helping to resettle the immigrants. I had forgotten this after 50 years when the country of Japan decorated me for my efforts. It was just something I had to do at the time to help my country people.

If my childhood was happy days, nothing to brag on, my teenage years were pretty colorful, helping everybody. I translated for the *Issei,* made them happy. We also had entertainment, silent movies, and began a number of important groups at this time.

My wife, Haruka, was born in Sacramento; we were married

in 1927 at the Florin Buddhist Church, the first wedding cele-
brated there. She helped me in my operation. A strong woman
physically, she can outwork me and is the backbone of my
present business.

I didn't have an education but I wanted my children to have
one. My father always stressed the need for higher education.
I didn't have a chance to get mine, but I learned both languages, which made me real handy to help others out. My
children went to school in Sacramento; the older ones attended Japanese school too, but it's all forgotten now. They
can't speak Japanese, but they can understand me when I
holler.

Sasaichi Sunada and Shikiyo Sunada, the parents of Haruka
Sunada

15

James, 24½, and Haruka, age 18, in the wedding portrait

In Sacramento before the evacuation, we had all the modern conveniences for a rural area of that time. We used butane gas, had an icebox, a washing machine, even a grand piano. We had 20 years of good times. We weren't rich in money, but we did have conveniences in the house. I had a Buick car and was doing all right.

James Imahara, age 20

I was president of a lot of corporations and helped to form one of the strawberry associations to pool our berries and sell them together. I was manager of the Northern California Berry Association, comprised of 100 or so farmers. We sent carloads of berries to the northwest markets, and our grapes went to New York, Chicago and other markets in the east. There were four Japanese-American strawberry shipping companies, representing nearly 200 farming families. One peak year our area shipped 129 carloads of berries to the Pacific Northwest. Most grape shipments were handled by white fruit shipping companies.

There was no profit in grapes; everything was cheap. The Japanese just barely made a living. The poultry business was more colorful and permitted quicker money; we sold up to 200 chickens a week at the Sacramento Flea Market. I was president of it, and my daughters May and Flora worked there as cashiers.

We had a colorful life, a very happy life. I was doing well at business and helping everybody. That was the saddest thing after the evacuation, the end of these ordinary days of youth. My biggest headaches came after the war and camp life.

In Sacramento, I was farming, president of the agricultural co-op, involved in everything. We had lots of community activities. I was secretary of the Northern California Farms Co. for 10 years, bookkeeper for two; prior to 1940 I took over the management of the association.

I was also president of the Young Men's Association, a sort of cultural exchange society in which the members exhibited great sincerity about learning and advancing themselves. As a teenager I was secretary of the Florin Investment Company, which purchased the land for our church; the older members ran the church as I was too young, but without my help to form the corporation, they couldn't have bought the land or built the church.

In my young days, I was also interested in Kendo, a Japanese martial art of fencing with bamboo sticks. My father's skill was Judo. Now I have a formal Japanese garment and sword, the real McCoy. In the Young Men's Association, we

18

advanced the hearts and minds and bodies; one without the other will not do, as all are essential. We also had another group to study agricultural techniques and keep up with the latest advancements, and a purchase co-op to buy rice and provisions together.

It was during this time that I was able to help the *Issei* so much. They would come to me for help with their problems leasing land, purchasing cars or equipment. They couldn't speak English well, asked me to interpret. I was glad to help out.

The agricultural co-ops helped us to sell strawberries by making contracts with buyers. We sold in carload volumes. We had over 200 acres of berries, which had to be sold quickly during the season. The Florin co-op normally handled three and four carloads daily, with about 2000 crates per car. I had learned how to manage the co-op when my father, who had been a director, got too old and would send me in his place.

If we had a buyer from the Pacific Northwest, I had to go and negotiate with him, make a contract. We had no money, so we had to get an advance; this procedure was customary. When the price went down, we had to call the buyer and re-negotiate the price; when we couldn't agree, we had to get an arbitrator to help settle things. The price was always very cheap, like 80¢ per flat of 24 pints of berries. We had to bear the expense of crates, baskets, labor; the grower made nothing. We had to sell at the peak of the season.

The Japanese farmer had a rough time. We had to borrow money to get started, then we'd get paid and pay back our loans, had to repeat the whole thing and borrow again next season. We were at a disadvantage, in the same boat every year, barely making our living. But I managed to help the *Issei* lease land and market their crops. In 1939 I managed the Elk Grove Berry Growers Association; there were 3 or 4 companies competing, but we topped them that year.

I was about the first in our community to buy a tractor for the farm, a crank tractor with steel tires. Everyone else had a horse and buggy, but I had my Fordson tractor. My first truck was a crank Ford, no self starter, with the brake in back. It took

19

awhile to start it, and with only 22 horsepower, it had to be pushed up inclines.

This was my situation before the war. That was what I had to lose, and what I did lose.

James and Haruka, with first child, May, 1928

As for Japanese-American relations, we know the conflict, but not what caused it. Japan was a small nation, wanting to expand through Manchuria; there was always fighting with the border army. Japan needed arms and war materials, was buying scrap iron from America, but an embargo stopped the sales in the late 1930's. Perhaps America feared that someday with our scrap iron Japan might make guns and come to this country.

Discrimination against what the West Coast called the yellow peril was rampant. The Japanese were good in horticulture, agriculture. Japanese strawberries and grapes were better than the white farmer's, because we had the interest, had to make our living. Japanese produce would thus sell first. The buyer wanted good stuff, regardless of the farmer's color. White farmers turned against us when our goods sold first; they got together with the politicians, denied us land. Jealousy and greediness were behind the 1913 Alien Land Act. The politicians and farmers wanted to keep California white. The Japanese slogan was to keep California green. We wanted to farm.

When war broke out, a Jap was a Jap, regardless of citizenship or country of birth. There was no distinction between *Issei, Nisei,* Japanese. It was like "Rawhide;" we were treated like cattle, driven not with whips but with guns and bayonets. "Round 'em up and move 'em out, get out of here, we don't need you; get out of service, etc., this is a white world!"

First came the Chinese Exclusion Law, then it expanded to all Orientals. When the Japanese came later, there were exaggerated fears of yellow peril. General John L. De Witt, Commander of the Western Defense Command during the war, was empowered by President Roosevelt to declare military areas on the West Coast and to exclude from them any and all persons. De Witt said "yellow is yellow, get them all out." It was a time of hysteria. Then came the army, "get 'em out of the West Coast," and 110,000 persons were penned up. Not Germans or Italians, who were at war too, only the Japanese. After four years in the camps, it was "get out of camp, we don't want you!"

James, Haruka and four oldest children

There were rumors of trouble for years. The anti-Japanese discrimination had been building through 1900, 1920, 1924, with anti-alien laws. Japanese could not purchase land, or lease land for long periods. Everything was piling up. Japan was expanding; there were so many people there, the space was getting too small for all the people. Japan needed to expand, was expanding militarily, which led to conflict with the U.S. We all said sometime we have trouble but nobody wants war.

The Roosevelt cabinet was putting pressure on Japan, but still thought she couldn't strike the U.S. 5,000 miles away. Even Hawaii was 3,000 miles. They said Japan hadn't the striking power. Then 250 planes came and struck Pearl Harbor. What made Japan strike is my question. There is a reason but nobody knows it. It is not my position to explain the war, but I know a lot.

I heard of the attack on December 7, 1941, on my car radio. It was a big shock. Martial law was declared. Japanese were put under curfew, could go only so many miles. There was no traffic; everyone stayed inside. All assets of the Japanese were frozen, and all Japanese people were termed enemy alien, even though three-fourths of them were American born. All Japanese were classified together.

Then came Roosevelt's evacuation orders, Executive Order 9066. All Japanese had to leave the West Coast and go inland.

It was a time of great confusion and turmoil.

When the Evacuation Orders came, San Francisco, Los Angeles, Terminal Island and all the places right on the coast had to get out within hours, the shortest times. With 24-hours notice to evacuate, these Japanese residents had to leave everything behind. They were so confused. Where to store belongings, where to go?

It was about January 1942 that the mass evacuation orders arrived in Sacramento. We had until the end of May to go, one of the last to go since not on the coast. Some refugees from coastal areas came to Sacramento to stay in the Japanese Hall, but it was burned.

It was a dark age. We couldn't see what was coming. All

23

110,000 Japanese were confused. I was about the oldest *Nisei*, so the army gave me a warden armband, the privilege to help with the others. The older Japanese immigrants spoke little English; as the oldest *Nisei*, I was fluent in both languages, so I could travel anywhere to help with the others.

Our cash was soon spent, since our assets had been frozen. I had to help friends get food and settle things. I was free to help the others, the old *Isseis*. I used to be a reporter for three newspapers until publication stopped; I had reported as a volunteer, paid only by a subscription to the paper, on our section's weddings, graduations, and so on. So I was used to talking to people and spreading the news, but everything stopped with Pearl Harbor.

The Japanese leaders, the president of the Japan Association, the minister of the Buddhist church, were rounded up by the FBI and put into detention camps. Fathers were separated from their families. Anyone involved in Kendo or Judo was considered loyal to Japan. I was involved, but was an American citizen, so they couldn't put me in detention camp then.

I left my property in Sacramento in charge of a good American friend. I had a small mortgage, $3000, which the bank took up and foreclosed on. Later I could have regained it but I didn't want to go back to California. My house was looted, then burned down. I could have picked up the pieces, I guess, but I was so sickened by what had happened. That's how much they hated Japanese.

The Axis like Germans and the Italians were not interned. Because of the yellow peril hysteria, the Japanese were the only ones interned. De Witt said "Jap is Jap, should be eliminated, don't come back."

I lost all my property that I had worked on for 20 years. From nothing but a hayfield I had developed vineyards and strawberry fields. In the camps we would raise our own food, chickens, hogs and vegetables. After the war, the government offered to pay for relocation. After the way my parents had been treated, I would not go back to California. My house and property were gone. I had nothing but 9 children and a wife.

I started all over. We all did. The Japanese spirit is going to

24

grow, wherever it is. It's all in the heart. Look at modern Japan after being bombed out. You cannot keep the Japanese spirit down; it will start growing. I feed good about telling this. I feel so relieved. This is the first and last time I've told it. I'm glad to have the opportunity to tell it. I could have written it in Japanese, but maybe not so well in English.

After Pearl Harbor, they told us to evacuate, so the Japanese did just as told. We left Sacramento on May 30, boarded a train south. We were kept in a horse stall on the fairgrounds in the Fresno Assembly Center, then shipped by train to Arkansas, where we were surrounded by barbed wire, sentry posts, machine guns. The government said this was to protect us, but the machine guns were pointed in. The guns pointed right to me. That was a fact. Something in my chest boils when I talk about this. I hope this will be the last time. I'm not a violent person, but I get excited about this.

Sacramento, not on the coast, was the last to go. At least we had more time than the others. We were ordered to carry all we could, leave the rest. We did. Mama had a beautiful bridal kimono, antiques, the grand piano. She left it all, took only important papers and bedding and her cherished family photograph albums. The children carried their share, even the four and five-year-olds. We were no longer Imaharas then, we were numbers.

We lost our identity, were given dog tags. Everything had to be put in duffel bags with our number stencilled on. We each carried two duffel bags to camp; these had our numbers and names on them, and I saved them to give to my children later as mementoes.

When we were ordered to evacuate from Sacramento the end of May, we knew we would be sent to the Fresno Assembly Center. We gathered at Florin Station, about 600 of us, since some had already been evacuated. I was a warden, had to check off names.

It was early in the morning when we gathered at the station. I took our belongings to the station in my truck, which a white friend then took home for me. We had sold our tractors and equipment at a fraction of their value.

Mrs. Imahara and children, Camp Rhower, Arkansas

I remember the big black train. We had to put the window shades down so the public wouldn't see us.

We lost everything but our family photographs. When we got on the train I had a black bag with important papers, which disappeared. Mama was most concerned about the family albums; she left her wedding kimono and the best dishes, but took the album when we evacuated. This was priceless to her, so I'm proud to have it.

At the Fresno Assembly Center, there were already many evacuees, many thousands of people, all in these temporary quarters. The buildings were in the form of barracks. There was a long latrine with holes and water running under it which scared the children. The bath houses separated the sexes but there was no privacy. It was all temporary, like the relocation.

We had army cots made of wood with canvas. For a mattress, we were given a sack, which we filled with hay. It was comfortable at first, but soon hollowed out. That's where "hit the hay" and "hit the sack" come from. These had to be restuffed periodically. After all the furniture we had at home, it was quite a change.

26

View of barracks, Camp Rhower, Arkansas, 1944

We were at Fresno about four months. In October we were sent to Arkansas. In Fresno I was a block manager, and had to provide a lot of help for the old people. They did not speak English, so I translated for them.

We all had a very bad feeling, but there was no use expressing it. We were not happy, but what can you do with the army watching. Mama went to Fresno expecting our ninth child, and had the baby there. She was well treated. There were Japanese doctors for the sick. All the care was provided by interned Japanese doctors.

In camp, most workers were paid from $12 to $16 a month. As councilman and block manager, I received $19 monthly as a professional, like the doctors and technicians. Mama had so many children to take care of, she couldn't work, but our oldest daughter May did some typing and was paid. We went to the canteen, and could order things from Sears or Montgomery Ward, usually the old stuff they couldn't sell.

In Arkansas, there was an old general merchandise store where we were permitted to shop on certain days. We cleaned out all the old unstylish inventory. America ran out of leather and was making imitations, but we bought all the old pre-war leather shoes. The United States and Russia were on good terms. Russia wanted butter, the U.S. was eating margarine. Russia refused imitation leather, so the American people had to use it. They needed Russian help so sent the best goods to them.

What I'm saying is not fiction. I don't make up. We don't talk this out in my family, so a whole generation doesn't know. This is my experience, not from a book. With my age I can see a little farther than the rest of them, even though I made lots of mistakes.

At Fresno, there were no materials for improvements. We made out with what we had. We sat on apple boxes. The government didn't supply anything but cot, hay, mattress cover. We all did our best.

The Japanese say, *"Shikataga Nai,"* which means what can you do under the circumstances. At Fresno Assembly Center there was no barbed wire, but there were sentries. At camp in Arkansas, we made our own furniture.

When the war broke out, short-wave radios, guns, knives, weapons and cameras were called contraband, were not allowed in camp. In Sacramento before the evacuation, all weapons were confiscated; I had a shotgun, .22 automatic revolver and a short-wave radio, all of which were taken. My father had a Japanese sword, which we dropped in the well. With no radios, we had no war news, only rumors and what our American friends told us. We had no way of knowing in camp, as we had no access to firsthand news.

Always at every point we had American friends who were kind to us. Many Americans saw the evacuation as unnecessary. It was the army brass who thought it was necessary. Many Americans were against the evacuation order. We were told we were put in camps for our protection, but Arkansas had barbed wire and sentries in watchtowers and machine guns. They were pointed in, not for protection. Some of the kids would dig holes under the fence to get out for a little while, but not the adults.

In the relocation center at Fresno there were many old bachelors, former migrant laborers with no families, who spoke no English. Many of them were feeble and sick. They wanted my help. As block manager in the camp, I was able to assist them.

I would later be decorated by Japan for my help to these people during the turmoil of the evacuation, and also for my earlier work. The decoration was a very great honor, being usually reserved for *Issei*, Japanese nationals, and I was a *Nisei*, a Japanese-American. I don't know how the Japanese consulate found out about my work. I went for two interviews at the consulate afterward. I think the honor came not just from my helping and translating but also from my active youth when I helped start lots of organizations through schools, churches and youth groups. I helped to build all those organizations. The consulate found out I was helpful to the *Issei* at the time they needed help, and that I was a good citizen; they were very particular to check to make sure I was not against the law. My checkup was good, no violations. They found that, as the oldest *Nisei* around, I had come in pretty handy.

Rhower Camp, 1944

29

I was notified by telegram from the Japanese Ambassador in Washington that I was to be honored. At the annual New Year's party at the Consulate in New Orleans, there was a big feast and a presentation ceremony. My decoration was presented by the Consul General, Heihachi Mochizuki, on behalf of the Emperor and people of Japan. All 200 members of the Japan Club were present. Along with the award was given the privilege of meeting the Emperor of Japan at a future date.

I had gone to Japan in the fall of 1977, and I received my decoration on New Year's Day 1978. Thus I had three big things in that year: my 50th wedding anniversary, my first trip to Japan, and my decoration by the government of Japan. It was a big year for me.

After Fresno came the order to go to Arkansas, to the Jerome and Rhower camps. Each had a capacity of about 10,000 occupants. From the Assembly Center, we were sent to Jerome; then German prisoners were sent there, so we were sent to Rhower.

Internee lumberjacks cutting wood, James at left rear

We went to Arkansas by train. My littler daughter Lily raised the shade passing through Oklahoma to look at the Indians. But mostly we were treated like cattle, not allowed to look outside. It was a secret military movement.

It was a long trip to Arkansas, four days and five nights. It was a hard trip with 8 children, aged 15 on down to an infant still nursing.

In Jerome, Arkansas, the train stopped in front of the camp. There was no station, just a lot of unfinished barracks. All were temporary buildings, on concrete block piers. Black tar-paper covered the outside of the buildings, which were long, about 100 feet.

The buildings were divided into sections. As we were the biggest family, we got a bigger section. We had two rooms. Our furnishings consisted of cots and a wood stove. We had to cut our own wood. I was a lumberjack. We had straw mattresses. I had to make our own shelves, closet, furniture. Mama made a pretty good carpenter too. All furniture was made by the evacuees.

We had one or two electric lights. We hung sheets or quilts for privacy between beds. Everything was open otherwise. There was no privacy. The walls were thin boards, and we could hear the next families. We all tried our best to be good neighbors for the duration.

First I was a block manager, then a councilman, a liason between the army and the evacuees. I was paid $19 a month. I would present grievances. The evacuees behaved well, though. There was no violence. What could we do? We took it.

We had to go to other buildings for the latrine and the mess hall. The mess hall was great big, with long tables. My brother-in-law was a chef. We bought rice, raised meat and vegetables and chickens. We were self supporting for the duration. There was plenty of food, not the best but we were never hungry.

At home, I had been a charter member and president in the Florin district of the Japanese-American Citizens League, which was legally established around 1925 and helped express our loyalty to the U.S.; I was also a charter member of the

31

Sacramento JACL, organized in 1931. Before it became the JACL, it was called ALL, American Loyalty League. Although it was not too influential in my area around the time of the evacuation, because the leader was young, we all helped to calm down the people.

What else could we do? It was war, and we must take our government's orders. There is a book now called *Nisei—The Quiet American*. We were all quiet, and did as we were told. In camp, you couldn't express much. We followed camp rules and law, went by army rules.

I left camp for a short while to work in Chicago. Japanese who passed a loyalty check could go out to work. I went to the Edgewater Beach Hotel to work, then to International Harvester building tanks. After a year of work they said they couldn't hire me; the FBI checked me out and said I could work there, but I wouldn't go back. I was in Chicago two summers

Camp Rhower group portrait, including Imaharas

and winters, so I wasn't in the camp as long as Mama. Her story of life during my absence is at the end this book.

When I came into camp I was so tired, both physically and mentally. I was not even walking straight. Camp life was one of the most tiring and boring things I had ever experienced. I wanted to get away. I knew I'd have a hard time finding a job in Chicago, and maybe I shouldn't have gone. But to my self-ish way of thinking I had to get out; money wasn't the whole object. In camp we were paid for labor; kitchen help got $12 a month, jobs with more responsibility got $16, and managers, doctors and councilmen got $19. It provided spending money for the kids, didn't go anywhere.

Even in Chicago, we were handicapped, being Japanese. They looked down on us as enemy aliens, didn't distinguish between *Issei* and *Nisei,* just looked at the face and saw the same. I didn't like Chicago. All my life I had been a country boy and I still want to be one. You can take me out of the country but you can't take the country out of me. City life is not for me. I was born from the soil and I'll go back to the soil.

In 1945 came Hiroshima and Nagasaki. The bombing ended it. Japan made an unconditional surrender. All Japanese were shocked at the loss of face. The atomic bomb is the most terri-ble thing. America was the first to have it, but now 9 or 10 countries do. Someone will drop it on the U.S. and it will mean annihilation. Both countries will lose. We must try to prevent it. Russia is now going after Poland, wants Iran and Arabian oil. We'll be out of oil; that's Russia's plan.

When the war ended, I was called back to Arkansas. They said, "relocate, go any place you want to." We didn't have a place to go. I said, "HELL, California, I won't go back."

We were so confused at the war's end. Where to go? I inves-tigated New Orleans with my good friend, Mr. S. Sagawa from Fresno. We had been good friends in camp. He was older, gave me lots of good advice. We had a good, close relationship. We decided to try the South. Chicago was too cold; now here we are in Louisiana, the hottest state. I hate hot.

I regretted the move for years. I had a big family, no decent job, hard living, hot weather, being pushed around in New Orleans where we went as a displaced family. After the war, in New Orleans, I crawled and I cried.

We went to New Orleans in the fall of 1945. We shared our duplex with the Sagawas. Mama had managed all right in camp without her husband; she had good foresight and took up sewing. She opened a little alteration shop in New Orleans to supplement my salary. She is the backbone; she is strong inside. We got along.

There was no Japanese consulate in New Orleans right after the war, so we had no place to go for help. Just myself and my judgment to rely on. I needed a job to feed my family, and I got one. It was low paying, but I made a living. We were pushed around. We had no problem renting a house, though. People in Louisiana were not as prejudiced against Japanese as in California; lots of the blacks didn't know where Japan was or much about the war.

When we got out of camp, they had given us $25 a head to start over. We had very little, slept on newspapers for several weeks, but I got some boxes to make furniture. Soon we got some army surplus double-decker bunk beds.

We lived in a duplex on Warrington Drive near Pontchartrain Beach, and often went there after work. Once I was asked to step to the back of the bus, I was tanned so dark.

New Orleans was rough, rough days. My daughter May remembers that we were ostracized. Mama began sewing, made money for the household. She advertised by word of mouth, and had a little sign on the window, "Alterations by Mrs. Imahara." May wanted to quit school to go to work, but was told "we don't hire Japs." She went back to school and worked part-time. It was hard on the children. May worked as a salesclerk for $11 a week on Canal Street, and gave half of that to the family. May remembers that we thought positive wherever we went; "Boy, we had guts when you think of it," she says. On job applications by race she filled in "white."

We paid about $60 a month rent on Warrington Drive. That was big money at that time with nine children. My first job was at a hatchery. I had had a chicken business in California and always had a love of it. I worked at night at the Louisiana Hatchery tending the incubator. I didn't make much, maybe $50 a week, and I really didn't like it much. I travelled to work on the city bus. I had to walk to Elysian Fields to catch the bus, and made many changes; I didn't know about bus transfers, so at first I lost many nickels, which were like dollars to me now.

Then I bought an old Ford touring car. It was black and had no brakes. I had to get the girls to push it to start, since the batteries kept running down. It was a good thing I had a lot of strong girls.

Next I worked at a nursery specializing in indoor tropical plants. I was making $75 a week, good for that time. I was there about a year. I had a feeling then. I'm a horticulturist. I have a love of growing things, a love of the soil. I made cuttings from prunings. It was good experience.

We were in New Orleans about five years. Through gardening work I met a Jewish woman, Mrs. Philip Kroll, who asked me to move to Kenner to take care of her yard, saying she would furnish a house. Her husband helped me so much. He was a real gentleman. I named my son Philip for him. He was a generous person, gave us dishes to use.

The Krolls gave us a dairy barn to live in, since their country home had burned, then bought an old barracks which we tore down to build a house for us. I also did finishing carpentry work then, and started farming, working for Frank Jordano Farms in Kenner. I was a farm hand, working with cattle, helping with the hay, feeding the stock.

In Kenner I met Sheriff Clancy, and we became partners to grow celery. He was a fine person, but it didn't work out. The dirt was not suitable, wouldn't retain water. It was not fit for agriculture. We had no irrigation, and I hadn't known the condition of the ground. I was able to raise a truck crop of tomatoes, eggplants, peppers, mustards and turnips to sell in the French Market in New Orleans, but I never got the irrigation system Sheriff Clancy promised. We were partners on shares; 40% to the landowner for furnishing the land, seed and fertilizer, 60% to the farmer for the labor. We lived in a shack there and the kids went to school, but it didn't work out.

I never did like a situation like that. I had been independent and had had land all my life. Over here, the land and housing were somebody else's. I never liked that condition. I want to be my own boss. That's why I am where I am today. I'm an independent man. My father was, too. He didn't make much on his farm, but we were independent. I knew I would have to start my own business, put my own price on work. That's the way my business eventually came up.

In New Orleans, all our Japanese friends stuck together. It was all we had. Our social gatherings kept us together and kept our spirits up, our cultural interest up, kept our Japanese ties.

All the Japanese got together. We would celebrate most at New Year's. We'd talk about the past, where we came from. We didn't have to talk about the present because we all experienced it.

One by one people went back to California. My friend Mr. Tanouei raised tomatoes, made enough money to go back; he lost two sons in the service. When we were in the camp, the government drafted Japanese-American boys into the service. Many didn't come back. When one was killed, the parents were brought a yellow telegram. We were all afraid of the yellow telegrams. There was such grief at that time, you could hear the crying all over the barracks. In camp everyone knew everyone, we all grieved. They interned the parents but drafted the sons. The 100th and 442nd Battalions were mostly Japanese Americans, and they proved their loyalty in the most heroic ways. It was a terrible thing to confine the parents and draft the sons, but they all went, obeyed orders. With guns and barbed wire, you didn't disobey.

When so many of our Japanese friends moved back to California, we were left behind. It was hard times. We had no money, and I didn't want to go back. When I left Sacramento, I had in mind that I would not come back anymore. There was bad feeling, anti-Japanese sentiment. I saw what had been done to my parents. I still have that feeling inside.

At first there were only about 20 Japanese families in New Orleans. There were maybe 100 of us altogether. About 50 or 60 went back to California. There was only a handful left. Mr. S. Sagawa and his family went to Kenner, and so did some of the other families. We went to farm, like the others. We don't like city life. I'm a country boy, can't stand the city.

We had a common need to get together for parties on holidays. It was always the same group. That was all the social life we had. We Japanese stuck together and helped each other. I was the poorest with the biggest family. We are still close.

Now there are maybe 200 Japanese in New Orleans, from Japan. But we are the original ones. Now they're from big companies, coming and going, newcomers. We're the originals, still loving each other. We got together in 1976 and formed the Japan Club of New Orleans, made up of the originals. I was asked to be the first president; I tried to decline, but they persuaded me to accept the honor. After a year I resigned due to my age and distance from New Orleans, so I was made honorary president and still am.

We always have a traditional New Year's party at the residency of the Consul General. All the Japanese come. It's one of the biggest celebrations each year. Rain or shine, we all go on January 1. We have Japanese dancing. The club also sponsors lots of activities during the year, and publishes a newsletter. We have about 60 or 70 members, though we had 200 at one time. We make donations for educational purposes, and keep the Japanese unified.

It was through Sheriff Clancy that I met Mr. Henry Mills. I was making about $75 a week in Kenner. He promised me the same money, Mr. Mills did, plus a house and pickup truck if I would work as head gardener at Afton Villa plantation in West Feliciana Parish north of New Orleans. New Orleans was flat, you could see many miles. West Feliciana was heaven, with rolling hills. We all liked it. It reminded me of California. It's easy the way I speak of it. But there was a lot of suffering in New Orleans. But it's best forgotten. If I told you all the suffering, you'd have many pages.

Imahara family at Afton Villa. Front row: Irene, Jun, Philip, left to right. Second row: Lily, John, Walter. Third row: James, Haruka, Flora, Jane.

I fell in love with Afton Villa. Mr. Mills and his daughter Miss Dot had recently purchased the plantation and renovated the huge house. We moved there in 1950. Miss Dot had been a young widow whose husband had been shot down in France; she needed cheering up, so Mr. Mills bought Afton Villa for her. She soon married Wallace Percy and they had a baby to join her small daughter, Adelea.

The extensive gardens at Afton Villa had been laid out in the 1800's, but had been neglected for years. The grounds were a wilderness, a ruin. They gave me labor, a tractor, and built a cottage for me. I straightened out the gardens in the two years I was there. Afton Villa I think of as my second home, my home away from home. Miss Dot to this day remembers all the family working, the children alongside Mama and me.

I left for Baton Rouge in 1952. I began working for a nursery

James Imahara and son John at entrance to Afton Villa, 1951

owned by Fred Heroman, but I can't take orders. I started James' Gardening Service, work done on contract.

In the early 1950's I had two girls in college; in the late '50's I had three boys in college, one studying to be a doctor. Mr. Clayton Rutledge of St. Francisville, a banker, helped me; he let me have all the money I needed to educate my family. All the degrees, Clayton Rutledge helped get. He asked for no collateral, just said, "Mr. Imahara, I'll trust you." I paid it all back, too.

Mr. Davis Folkes, the West Feliciana representative to the state legislature for many, many years, helped when Flora was in college. She graduated from Kenner High School as valedictorian; it was a small class. She was rebellious; I applied the whip of love, not hatred. She was the best child after graduation, helped support us so the household got better. Flora went to Pelican Girl's State and got a small four-year scholarship; we borrowed money to cover her other expenses. My oldest daughter May borrowed $100 from the bank in Metairie on her name alone at age 17 or 18; I'll never forget that bank and the first time we were not turned down as "Japs."

Flora and Jane both went to LSU. As always, there was no money. We moved closer to Baton Rouge and lived in a shack. We got credit in the stores.

I knew I wanted all my children to get a higher education. In 1959 I had three in college; I won't do that again! My son John was brilliant. Walter changed his major from cars and girls to plants. He started at SLI and got into weightlifting, so no more girls; I paid for his brawn instead of his brain, but he is a good, gentle person and I have confidence in him as in all my children. John went to four years of medical school but didn't like to see blood. Japanese are very clever with their hands, but he wouldn't be a surgeon because of the blood. He had straight A's and graduated as salutatorian from Central High School, then asked me what he should do. I said be a doctor. I supported three years of pre-med, four years of med school, three years of internship. John said he had to be a doctor because his Papa said to be a doctor. Who listens these days? He was thrifty and studied hard.

When John graduated, he took his parents to California. I had no suit to wear, and the same shoes I'd had for 20 years. John gave me his old shoes and I bought a $75 Sears suit. He had saved everything. He drove us in his new six-cylinder car. John is a fine person. He knew we suffered to give him everything. I had no shoes, no good clothes, but my children had two pairs of shoes. We parents had nothing, but that was all we needed.

It was struggling days in the 1940's and 1950's. It was a struggle to get money; but we all had our health. Daily bread was my biggest concern. I worked, and kept working even after most people retire. I had my business and my health was good, so I kept going. I was insulted by the automatic Social Security check I got; I didn't retire until age 71. My daughter May says nobody in this family knows how to fish or relax. Most people can't wait to retire, but I kept on working.

The first land I bought in Baton Rouge I bought with borrowed money, four acres to start a nursery. I paid that all back, too, with interest. We're clear now, no debts. It wasn't until 1958 that I could buy the land. After years of driving an old truck, now I drive a new car. I've been through everything, but a person has to crawl before walking.

Some time after the war, in 1958, the government did pay some of the property claims of the Japanese, but only about 10¢ on the dollar. This was nothing to what we lost. We lost everything, our farms, our crops, our homes, our possessions, our identities, years of our lives. We lost everything, but we had enough to start again, made a down payment on a house and land. I was lucky in a way; I came to Baton Rouge at a good time. Baton Rouge grew, and I grew.

While the Claims Act was being negotiated, I wrote Washington monthly. We lived in a rent house, hoping for the money and a new life. Always next summer it was coming. Forms to fill out, government trying to compromise, negotiate claims. We just got a fraction. Our claim was over $100,000; we got $17,000. It wore us out, trying every means. Gully and Poor Realtors had a house, we needed a down payment, hoped the money would come in. Mr. Gully called Washington for Congressmen Morrison's help. There were tons of claims filed, maybe mine was on the bottom of the stack, but Congressman Jimmy Morrison was so influential that in a week the money was coming.

We were happy to get it. We bought a house and a barn with it. I removed the fences, graded, put in drainage, bought a Ford tractor, fixed it just the way I wanted, put in garden grass and started my business from there. It was just me and Mama, and the boys on weekends, that was James' Gardening Service.

When we left Afton Villa, I bought a greenhouse from Mr. Mills. He had put it up for me. It had cost $2000, but he sold it to me for $500 and moved it. Mr. Mills had also bought me a brand new pickup truck in my name. See how he trusted me? When I left, I signed it over to Miss Dot's husband, Wallace Percy. They had confidence in me. When I left Afton, I had no transportation; Miss Dot endorsed a loan of $500 to buy a truck, which I paid back. They helped me in many ways. Mr. Clayton Rutledge at the bank also trusted me, asked for no security.

After James' Gardening Service, I started Pelican State Nursery. When Walter, my son, came back from the army, we named it Imahara Nursery and Landscape Company, Inc. When I was by myself, one person, it was wobbly; when Walter came back, we had two legs, stronger; then my daughter May joined us, three legs like a tripod, much stronger. This is the Japanese way. One is weak, two are still weak, but you can't break three arrows.

We were lucky, too, because the time was right. Baton Rouge was growing. There was new housing, lots of building, new chemical plants being put in. There were many new settlers coming to the town. Garden clubs would ask me to lecture; I did it as a volunteer, to help my name to become known. Soon the name *Imahara* was recognized. This is a Japanese name; I'm so proud that I'm Japanese. In Baton Rouge if you ask what's Japanese, the answer is Imahara; that's what Baton Rouge has identified as Japanese for 30 years. There were no other Japanese in Baton Rouge at the time I started my business, only us. Later, there were many war brides, but they were rather unknown, and I had a business and was known.

I made many donations which made the Imahara name stand out, too. These made me real happy, the donations to churches. I gave all the landscaping for Mama's church, the Parkview Baptist Church, when the new building was put up. The old church, too; it had not a blade of grass, and I landscaped it, gave it all I had. It was my contribution from here, my heart. I did all the work myself. The landscaping for the new church cost $10,000, all a donation. I also did the landscaping for several Baptist churches in St. Francisville, Calvary Baptist and First Baptist, and several in Baton Rouge. Mama is a Baptist; so are several of my children.

When I started the nursery, it was slow at first. I put up a greenhouse, then bought several greenhouses from a nursery closing in Metairie. I started with cactus first; they're easy to propagate, and can be sold for 50¢ apiece. Philodendron too you can start from practically nothing. That's the trick in nursery, to make cuttings from pruning. Now they buy a lot, don't work as hard, but my way is the profit way, the hard way.

Before turning Pelican State into Imahara's, I had to wait for Walter to get out of the service. These were hard years. My second son John was studying to be a doctor. Several other children were in college. They were struggling years. I borrowed, borrowed. It took a long time to pay back. I needed a hand, depended on Walter and his horticulture degree. He gave everything. The nursery to me is his. We needed each other, a combination of my years of experience and his degree. Walter learned from books, but he is a good worker.

When Imahara's Nursery and Landscape Co. opened for business in 1968, we had a 30×72-foot building on Florida Blvd. Slowly Pelican State was phased out and in 1970 Imahara's was incorporated with my son Walter as president and my daughter May as treasurer. We grew and expanded over 3½ acres on Florida Blvd., adding more buildings, patios, greenhouses, parking areas, foliage and production houses, as

Imahara family in front of Imahara Nursery at Golden Wedding Anniversary celebration for James and Haruka Imahara, 1977

well as a fresh and silk flower florist department and home gardening supplies.

Soon the whole 3½ acres was needed for the retail business, so 4½ acres on Old Hammond Highway was purchased and the entire landscaping department was relocated there in 1979. There we could accommodate the homeowner wishing to do his own landscaping as well as larger commercial or residential bid jobs.

When we bought the land on Florida Blvd. for our retail store business, it was a hard decision. May had to come in from Georgia to be secretary-treasurer. She's the boss now. She worked 8 days a week for years. She wore herself out, but did get her share of the business, now she and her husband Sam are partners with Walter.

We made a success at starting over, but it was not easy. I'm a human being. I have the bitterness, but I had to buckle down. I said no use crying over spilled milk. I said I must leave it all behind, must educate my children. I went straight forward to this new life, where I am today.

Bygone is bygone. I don't look back and regret. I have no regret. It was a hard struggle, especially with my big family, going to a place where I was unknown. But the people were good to me, gave me support.

I am humble. It's the Japanese way. I give glory to the other person. I take, but give a little more than what I take, same in business. I clean up after work, take away the trash; others don't give any more than they are paid for. In nursery, I would give a little more. My policy and the secret of my business is being humble and giving more. When I was paid, I would give a free plant, my gift. I dress for work, never dress up; same when I work as when I borrow money. I represent myself, just myself, I don't camouflage.

We did the inside and outside landscaping at Cortana Mall, the biggest landscape job for Imahara's and the biggest landscape job ever let in Louisiana. I also did Coca Cola's landscaping and maintenance, and did landscaping for Russell Long, Blanche Long, Douglas Manship (I called his yard Manship Park!).

45

James and Haruka Imaḥara at Golden Wedding Anniversary, 1977

I had many Jewish supporters who gave me their business so my business could grow, also lots of doctors. I have a lot of American friends who helped me along. One of the bankers said that when Mr. Imahara came to Baton Rouge, the gardens got beautiful. Maybe that's my contribution.

I'm lucky to be here. I owe great gratitude to the people of Baton Rouge. They're all nice to me, supported my business. I have numerous friends among the older generations.

I crawled, but I'm on my feet now, standing up. I owed this to my people, my ancestors. We walked the same narrow right path.

I'm a happy man now. I make *haiku*. These are 17-syllable poems of the Japanese spirit. Who is the Japanese? Just like the cherry blossom in the morning sun. From the naked tree come blooms; then all petals drop, and the bloom is gone. We may have fight, but then are friends again.

Haiku are seasonal poems; spring and autumn are best time to make them. *Haiku* I have made about trickling water and minnow, a log forming a natural round bridge, a soft breeze, walking on leaves, the sound of water, crepe myrtle hanging low with rain or heavy with dew. I studied *haiku* as a teenager. You must have something strike you, like candlelight when the electricity goes out and a firefly comes to the window. It comes to me, and I am so happy the lights went out and the shades were up.

The *haiku* is something that strikes you. During my dark age, from about age 40 to 60, *haiku* didn't come. I was too busy, didn't have the time or peace needed. Now life is a little peaceful and I am free again, so *haiku* come back. All I have now is my *haiku* and my carving.

I have several *haiku* published each month. You can read the poems and tell whether the author is male or female. The mood is expressed through the *haiku*, feelings are shown which differ even on the same subject.

One I just wrote is

My good friend passed
He left me a memento which is a wristwatch.

恍々と
Ko Ko to
Brightly

吾が道照す　秋の月
waga michi terasu
shine my path
aki no tsuki
Autumn moon

土のノド
Tsuchi no kudo
Stove made of mud

ママが炊く
mama ga mama taku
Mother makes rice
ママの味
mama no aji
rice is so tasteful

山荘の
San so no
At the cabin

曙告げる
akebono tsugeru
early morning call
鶏の声
tori no koe
a rooster

HAIKU is a short Japanese poem, consisting of 17 syllables in order of 5-7-5.

俳句 喜翁

HAIKU by Ki-o (Happy Old Man)

春立ちて
Haru tachi te
It's Springtime

山は緑で
yamawa midori de
trees are green

花と鳥
hana to tori
flower and bird

一条の
Ichi jo no
A streak of

チムネの煙
chimune no kemuri
smoke from chimney

屋根の霜
yane no shimo
frost on roof

49

I did have a happy life. My family, up to war time, was all together. We had no money, no radio or TV, but we were happy. Then came sad days and my struggle. I have educated my children and now all are free, so I'm free again.

I crawled, but I'm on my feet now, standing up. I've done everything, so I have no regrets. I did not make a million, but I have enough to do. I got tired working on my first million, so I'm going to work on my second one first. It's supposed to be easier. I'm going to take a shortcut.

My life was hard until age 65, then I turned the horseshoe around and things got better. I really brag that I've got good children. We're close, all together. We've been through so much. Mama says that's where the children got their sense of security, from all of us being together, living day by day. Mama's sister once asked for our two daughers to live with her; Mama said if we die, we die together, if we live, we live together. We had hard times, but Mama and I were thankful all our children stayed together for better or worse. Mama says she thinks it was the war that made our family so close. My daugher May remembers that we were all so vulnerable in those years after the war; if anybody had said one unkind word, we would grovel at their feet, she says. But we each did our own special thing in our own way, no one in the family more than others. We all helped each other.

It's the same thing in my ancestral family. We love each other, we help each other.

It goes back to the old family way, the Spartan way of upbringing. Now we appreciate the firm way. Everything was black or white, yes or no, day or night; it was all clear. Now everything is bigger, more trouble, more headache. I'm not a perfect father, but I have my way of doing it. I think my father was right; I follow his footsteps. I was rebellious in my young days, but now I appreciate it. I was a smart alec, but I found out I didn't know anything. It took me a long time to be mature. Some people mature later, and you have to give them time.

One of my favorite pastimes now is wood carving. I have made hundreds of carvings to give away. I put my heart and

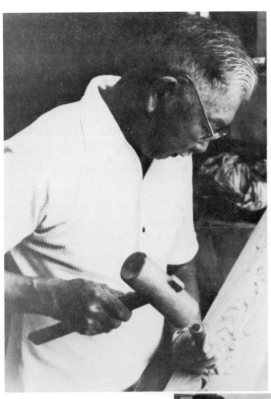

Above, James Imahara works on wood carving for granddaughter Linda. Right, he is shown with finished carving, a favorite which translates "God is Love."

soul into all this. I carve Japanese words or poems onto boards. I use three chisels, ⅛″, ¼″ and ½″. After I draw the design, I drive the chisels with a mallet to outline the curves. I have two mallets, one heavier and one lighter. Some pieces I work on for over a month. The skill is all in my hands, from my years of experience using my hands.

I'm very happy in my workshop. I concentrate all my energy into my chisel and mallet. I also collect iron pots, wagon wheels, old iron kettles, pot belly stoves, pumps. My biggest collection is horseshoes. I must have 250 of them. My philosophy has changed, though. I'm not superstitious. I have it all, depend on the Lord, not luck, so I can hang my horseshoe upside down, open.

On one of my wood carvings with Japanese figures, I hung a horseshoe. Someone told me it was upside down, the horseshoe by the name Imahara. But I used reverse psychology. I wanted luck in my days of struggle, but my luck didn't hold. When the horseshoe was up, it didn't hold luck. Reversed, open, with the Lord helping it is now holding luck. But now I don't need luck; I've got all the luck in the world. The Lord's way is to do things the natural way; the horseshoe is open but is holding luck in. I've got everything in the world and am the happiest man in the world.

You might say I have two countries, and I am a product of both. The United States is my father country, Japan is my mother country. Thanks to both of them, we made it.

I'm a Buddhist. When my mother came to the United States in the early 1900's, she was in a strange country, lonesome for her family, isolated by language barriers. When she carried me, she used to say, "I put my faith in Buddha, *Namua-Mida-Butu.*" I inherited this from her even before birth. This was an internal influence, not an outside one; I was born into Buddhism, and I'm going with that. My first schooling was in the Buddhist parsonage after American school in 1909. Each afternoon I was taught the 3 R's in the Buddhist way; this was the only school I knew.

I have relied on Buddhism all my life, and it has helped me to stick to the one straight road, just the way my parents and

Buddhism taught me, allowing no mistakes. I have followed in their footsteps in the Buddha's way.

Buddhism originated in India many thousands of years ago. A prince born into a royal Indian family became dissatisfied with the way things were running, with sickness, old age, death. He left the royal castle, where he could have had everything, and went into the woods to meditate. At age 37, he was enlightened, found the way of living, and spread the gospel to the country people. It is an old, old religion which spread from India through China, Korea and Japan.

We attended the Buddhist church in Sacramento, and my daughters went to Sunday school there; we had one in my house, too. I wanted my children to follow in my footsteps in the Buddhist way. But after Sacramento, there was nothing, no Buddhist church, so they slowly converted to Christianity, Mama too. She was born in a Buddhist family, but after there was no church, she converted and was baptized.

This does not mean there is a split in my family. A tie is here, but we are of different religions. This is uncontrollable. I can't tell Mama, religion is her privilege. I have my way, she has hers. My children know Buddhist teachings, but religion is something you must wake up to yourself. I have to accept that. It's their life.

Besides my *haiku*, I have another special Japanese art, *bonsai*. *Bonsai* means dwarf tree. I have one of the most outstanding examples of *bonsai*. It is a hugh sago palm in an 8-foot-diameter pot which is hundreds of years old like the palm. I call it the biggest *bonsai* in America. I dedicated that *bonsai* to my parents and to my in-laws in honor of their memory. It is at my nursery, but it is not for sale at any price; it is one of my treasures. I selected and planted the beautiful tree myself.

Even after I'm dead that *bonsai* will stay there in memory of the *Issei* pioneer families in this country. They cleared and cultivated to make the land productive. I owe them much, so it's my dedication for all the *Issei*, but especially for our parents. I'm a good writer in Japanese, but not in English, so I have written their memorial in an 8-foot pot with a beautiful palm.

I want to emphasize that I was happy in my youth. I grew up with no worries. I had my father and mother behind me, didn't know what worry was. I had no luxuries but I was happy.

I'd like to go back to that day. It's past, but I have the memory. My children's memory is fading, though, and my grandchildren don't know. When I was born, it was horse and buggy and oil lamps; then crank Ford automobiles. All the changes I've seen in the past 70 years, I don't know what's going to become of the world. We're just at the peak now. I'd like to go back to the old days again, though.

Some people would think I was crazy. I'm a pioneer son, have the memories. Everything was so peaceful in those days. There was no crime; no one ever locked their house. Now you have to have two or three locks and you still have a break-in. It's a crazy world now. I liked the old days. I've seen an awful lot, come a long way. I've seen three major wars, the Russian-Japanese War, World War I and World War II. War is hell, a terrible thing. Now there is the bomb and it will be the finish. All the big countries have atomic bombs, military build-ups; the next war will be a quick one.

In October of 1981 I went back to Sacramento for a 40-year Evacuation Reunion. Most of the *Issei*, first generation Japanese immigrants, are deceased now; the average age of the *Nisei* now is about 65 or older. I had gone back before. I was 38 when I left California during the evacuation; after 22 years of struggle, I finally went back for the first time on borrowed money; even a wagon train wouldn't take that long. But my family came first, and I had them to feed, clothe and educate.

My first trip back to California was in 1964, 22 years after leaving. I went back after my son John graduated from medical school. I had had no money to go back before, but I had always dreamed of it, of seeing my land and my friends again. It was a slow journey by car and in prop planes, but I went back.

My sister May and brother Henry came to my daughter's house, brought fruit, lots of relatives, and we had a big party. I had limited time, but saw a few old friends. We had aged, but we could recognize each other. I was real happy. We went to San Francisco, where my son John saw his first Chinese and first learned that I could speak Japanese. I thought, California here I come; this is my state, the golden state. It was where I had been born, and my thoughts wandered back to the old days.

I had a warm welcome from friends still there. I went back to Sacramento, visited the old Sierra School, a grammar school where my daughter and I had both gone. I went back to my own land. The vineyard was gone, and it was back in the state I bought it in. The house was there then, but later burned. The big chicken house was there. Later 60 acres of this land was turned into a gravel pit. There was a rumor of deep gold, and afterwards, the property, my land, sold for a quarter of a million dollars. See the kind of loss we sustained? We got maybe 10% of its value.

When the war began, we were confused, upset, terrified; the future looked dark. This was my dark age. We didn't know if we'd have to leave, abandon our property. Then the order came, Executive Order 9066, and we all had to leave. Where we'd go, nobody knew. We were real miserable and hurt, didn't know who to blame. We were confused.

Then gradually, we began to see a little light. It happened, we had to face it, even if we felt it was unjustified. We were American citizens; nothing happened to Axis descendants, but we were relocated just because of physical appearance. We had resentment, but what could we do. I will never forget the FBI checking on me in Sacramento because my chicken incubator had blinking lights; they checked to see if I was sending signals, because the lights had been spotted by planes.

After we were released from camp, it was a struggle to find a way to live, feed the family, pay the rent. My mind was full of misery and resentment, but this faded away in the busyness of the time. Once lost, it was gone, and there was no use crying over spilled milk. We had to start a new life, move forward. Look straight ahead, not back at what was gone. Japanese proverb: "Nana-korobi-yaoki," means 7 failures, then success the 8th try.

55

In my life I failed 7 times. On the 8th time, with the aid of heaven, I was lifted. It's like baseball, but with 7 strikes; on the 8th try, a home run. That's my life. I stumbled and fell 7 times; with the aid of Buddha, I was lifted to where I am now on the 8th try.

All my life I wasn't alone. I had the guidance of my father and mother, the Lord Buddha, and my ancestors to lead me. They were my guiding light. I had to go to the Lord for help and guidance. The business I couldn't have done myself. Mama was my partner; side by side we worked, and all the children helped. It was a family affair. Even the little ones worked. We built our own business.

My security and happiness I owe to my wife and the Lord. My prayer is: Thank you Lord Buddha, thank you father, thank you mother, thank you my daughter in heaven (she guided me), thank you my ancestors (they must have been good ancestors to have given me good health and never any trouble with the law), thank you my kinfolks, thank you all the people in the world who helped and gave me moral support, thank you Baton Rouge where the people are sure nice (I have had no enemy in my life, I hate no one: I have had differences of opinion but not hate; my father was an expert in Judo, the art of self defense, for protection, not to hurt others; the secret of Judo is don't get involved, but if cornered, give them one and walk away; I still have that in here; all my life I have made friends, I am a rich man in friends and past memories; I am all prepared, and if I hear one clear call, I'm going to answer); thank you for this USA, thank you great nation of Japan. I'm thanking everyone in the universe; now that I'm happy He can take me anytime—in the yard when I'm growing a flower, at the carving table carving "God is Love," the most beautiful words in the universe.

To the Japanese way of thinking, there are certain years that are most important. Age 37 holds the possibility for happiness; 77 is considered happy for man or wife, 88 is another celebration since very few make it, and at 99 a man has lived more than a full life.

Minezo Imahara, father of James, at age 75

Minezo Imahara, father of James, is shown in Sacramento, California, at the age of 75. With him are Lily and Walter, children of his son James, and a cousin, Norman Imahara (in overalls).

To make my life story possible, there were my children, all of them. Maybe one did a little more, but they all made it possible. Above all, there was my wife. All my sons- and daughters-in-law helped too, they are all my children. Even the grandchildren helped.

My oldest daughter May finished high school in the New Orleans public school system, then graduated from a business school. We encouraged her to finish high school rather than quitting to work, even though we were struggling. She worked after school at W. T. Grant and another clothing store as a saleslady and cashier. After graduation, she worked for a drug firm, and was transferred to Austin, Texas, as executive secretary with this firm. There she met Sam Kaga, a Japanese-American who had also been interned during the war. They married, had two children, travelled with his firm to Birmingham and to Georgia. Sam was a chicken sexer. Then they returned to Baton Rouge to become partners in Imahara's Nursery. May is the treasurer, and Sam is vice president.

Their daughter Christeen graduated from Tara High School as valedictorian, attended LSU in pre-med and graduated with a doctor's degree from LSU-Shreveport; she is a bone specialist, married to John Clack. Their second daughter Cathy graduated from Tara High, also with honors, went to LSU and graduated with a DVM from LSU School of Veterinary Medicine; she lives in New Haven, Connecticut, married Dr. Bill Ormsbee and will complete her residency in 1981.

My second daughter Flora graduated with honors as valedictorian of Kenner High School, had a scholarship from Pelican Girls State for 4 years at LSU, where she graduated in Landscape Design. She worked for a Baton Rouge firm, and met Ralph Yoshida from Hawaii, a Hawaiian-born Japanese attending Southeastern. They were married in Baton Rouge at Victoria Baptist Church. Ralph went to Emery Dental School, and after graduation went into the service and was sent to Germany. He was a major when he got out. Their first child was born in Georgia; the last three were born in Germany during their four years there. They went to California after discharge and Ralph opened his own practice. He is very successful. Flora, who worked and supported her husband during his training at Emery, is now a housewife whose major interest is in her family and in Christian work in San Jose.

I educated my girls. In Japan it was not customary to educate girls, but I said my girls need an education in case something happens to their husbands, so they can be independent. Flora has a profession but it's idle now, not needed. But she has it to fall back on just in case.

Flora and Ralph have four children. Diane, a graduate of the University of Hawaii, is in private graphic design; she is very artistic. Brian, who graduated from college in California, is now at Oral Roberts University in Tulsa in dentistry, after taking pre-dental courses at UC-Berkeley. Albert, the gentleman, is in physical therapy; at college he trained for Olympic swimming, and has taught swimming. Dean is the charmer, the carefree comic; he's in college in California.

Third daughter Jane graduated from Julius Freyhan High School in St. Francisville, then from LSU, majoring in education. She graduated in 1955, and became a teacher. She has taught the educable mentally retarded, first grade, and presently teaches third grade. She has been teaching nearly 30 years in Baton Rouge. She married Bill Wilson, a Baton Rouge native who graduated from LSU and was in education also. He's now assistant to the director of the School of Veterinary Medicine at LSU. Jane met him when he was the coach at a school where she was teaching. They have two children, Leslie, who is at LSU in Electrical Engineering, and Patricia Jane, a high school student.

Fourth daughter Lily met J. C. Metz in St. Francisville, married young and had seven children. She graduated from St. Francisville High through the GED program after marriage and six children. Then she started LSU while pregnant with her seventh child, and went for six years with no break except one semester off to have the baby. She graduated in December 1979 with a degree in Psychology. It took her a long time but she finally made it. That's my girl. I'm proud of her. After years of volunteer service and church work, she has her first paying job with the Council on Aging.

Lily and J. C.'s oldest daughter Linda graduated as valedictorian from SFHS, won a scholarship and graduated in math from La. Tech in Ruston. She married Bill Snyder, an electrical engineer with lots of degrees, and they live in Dallas, where she works at Texas Instruments. Joyce, the second daughter, graduated from SFHS and La. Tech, married John Roberts, and is working on a doctorate in Home Economics. Son Johnny graduated from SFHS and vocational school, is employed by Dixie Electric and is married to Tracy Martin; they have one son.

Lily and J. C.'s fourth child is Wanda Jo, who graduated from SFHS and is attending LSU in Landscape Design. Son Randy is a high school graduate; daughter Amy is very artistic, and Gaye is in elementary school.

My oldest son is Walter, who graduated from Istrouma High School and from SLU in Lafayette in horticulture. He was no honor student. His major interest in school was weightlifting, and he had an outstanding record. He dropped the girls for bodybuilding. When he got into weightlifting, he forgot all his other obligations. We paid for his brawn instead of his brain! It took him 5 years to finish college; he began the first year in engineering, then changed to horticulture. Walter went into the service and was stationed in Germany, where he met Sumi Matsumoto, a California Japanese who was teaching there. They were the only Japanese around. Sumi is very sweet and wonderful; I'm very lucky I got a daughter-in-law like her. They were married in Germany.

After the service, they came back to Baton Rouge and Walter became a partner in my Pelican State Nursery. We decided to branch out, bought land on Florida Blvd. which was very expensive then. We could hardly make the loan, but we began a whole new career. It started out as James Imahara Nursery, then James Imahara and Son, then Imahara and Sons, and then incorporated as Imahara Nursery and Landscaping Corporation.

61

Walter helped build up the nursery and continued his weightlifting career. His best friend, "Sarge," Paul Pendley, trained and encouraged him, and he took it to the heights of his career. He has a roomful of trophies, hundreds of them. During the most active part of his career, from 1956 to 1968, Walter was 9 times Southern AAU champion, 5 times National Senior champion, 6 times Louisiana State champion, Southern USA champion twice, Pan American Games titlist, National YMCA champion, and International Sport Competition Olympics titlist. He held many featherweight and lightweight records. We were all proud of his excellence in this gruelling sport. He travelled extensively with it, and he still coaches weightlifting. He won first place recently in California Middle Age Weightlifting.

Besides weightlifting, Walter has other special interests. He takes pride in helping landscape students, gives them special attention. He hires lots of college students to help them. Walter went through a hard time so he understands and wants to help today's students. That's the kind of feeling we have.

When I retired at 71, I sold my share in the business to Walter and Sam. We have continually expanded the business. Imahara Landscape Inc. on Old Hammond Highway is the second phase of the business, and does landscaping in other locations. The biggest job we've had was the landscaping, both exterior and interior, at Cortana Mall, calling for literally thousands of plants. Cortana was designed in New York, so we had to modify it a little. These young people sit at fancy tables in white collars doing the design, but we do the planting, we know what it will look like in the future. We mostly followed the design, even to the exact numbers of plants. But they ordered red maples; they are a northern plant. I said they would die, and they did. The architect got huge plants, and we had to prune them. I must have planted 70 or 80 oaks, and lost none of them. Everything came out just the way I planted. That's because of my experience; I know plants. The Cortana job was the biggest landscape job in Louisiana; we're still responsible for the maintenance there. We also landscaped Corporate Mall. The landscaping helped the business.

My next son John graduated from Central High School with honors. He was salutatorian. Two boys tied for top honors, but the white boy got the top one. John spent three years in pre-med at SLI, then graduated from LSU School of Medicine in New Orleans in 1964. He did his internship at Charity Hospital in New Orleans. John was one of the youngest (age 25 years) doctors to graduate in his class. In summers, he helped me at the nursery. After medical school, he was in the service four years during the Vietnam conflict.

John was a brilliant student who had uninterrupted schooling. I was without much money but had the courage to say to him, "Be a doctor." It was a financial struggle. At LSU Med School in New Orleans, he was scared about applying for funds, went for an appointment with a dean, and poured his heart out to the secretary; she told the dean, and he got the scholarship.

All my children had to struggle for money. Clayton Rutledge, the banker in St. Francisville, was the backbone of our efforts for education. Flora and Jane got scholarships through state legislator Davis Folkes. Lily got a BEOG grant. When Walter needed money, he won first prize in a contest by developing an orchid, which got him a scholarship.

John is a doctor but doesn't like blood, so now he's a San Jose psychiatrist. He did his residency at Los Angeles County General. He met his wife, Dwain, a South Carolinian, in California; she was a medical technician at the county hospital. After his residency John went to Vietnam as a major and was stationed in Saigon helping soldiers with problems. He spent much of his time in court due to drug abuse by soldiers. Back in this country he worked at a Veterans hospital in California until his discharge. John and Dwain were married in Hawaii while he was still stationed in Vietnam; Mama and I and Flora all went. They had a big reception later in California. They have two small sons, David and Scott.

My son Jun graduated from Woodlawn High School, attended Southeastern for two years, joined the army for four years, and went to California, where he graduated in Social Welfare from California State. He worked for years with juvenile delinquents for Los Angeles County. He married Carolyn and they have one son, Masaru ("Mas"). After 10 years in corrections Jun came back to Baton Rouge to work with the nursery for a short time. He helped with a lot of the hardest work and supervision when we did the Cortana Mall landscaping job, then went back to California, where he is with a motorcycle firm.

Daughter Irene graduated from Central and attended LSU. Thirty hours short of graduating in Landscape Design, she married Roland Diez, the boy next door. An LSU graduate in Architectural Design, he is in private practice in Bound Brook and Trenton, New Jersey. They have one son, Derek. Irene works with her husband in the family architectural consulting business, as well as with the Boy Scouts.

Philip, the youngest of my children, I call the Rebel since he was born in New Orleans. He graduated from Woodlawn High School and attended LSU and LSU-NO. He joined the navy for four years and was stationed in Seattle. When he got out, he graduated from the University of Washington in History. He has had various jobs, and is still single. He is good at specialized pruning. Most of my children are following in my footsteps and love to prune; horticulture is in the blood.

Education came first for my family. I think you must suffer to know the value of education. Now the children are born with silver spoons in their mouths, don't appreciate it. Children now are looking for a good time, don't see the value of education.

After all the children were educated, I went back to Japan. It was in 1977, a glorious year for me. That was my 50th wedding anniversary, the year of my decoration by the government of Japan, and my trip. We had a big party, and the children gave us some money toward the trip to Japan. I had always wanted to go there, to see my father and mother's country. Before, I didn't have the time or the money. But I wanted to see the country, to pay my respects to my Imahara memorial and the old ancestors' tombstones.

I speak fluent Japanese, so there was no language barrier.

I'd read about it all my life, but seeing is so different. I had great pride in my ancestry. First I saw Mount Fuji. It was a clear day, and you could see the top, the whole sacred mountain. We saw the memorial at Hiroshima, the shrines, the temples. The shrine at Kyoto was not bombed. There was glistening gold in the temple. The memorial honors all soldiers killed in all wars. Japan had its own god and considered the emperor of divine descent, so there are many temples. Every successful *shogun* dedicated his shrines or temples.

We were on the *Bonsai* Tour, to see *bonsai*. But to me the *bonsai* was secondary; I wanted to see Japan and my wife's folks. My own family was mostly gone, except for my nephew Richard who had a thatched roof house. Most of the roofs are tile now due to incendiary bombs. But I wanted to see the originals, the old Japanese ways. There are modern high rises there now, but I wanted to see the old Japan, how my parents lived before they came to this country, the fireplace in the floor in the middle of the room for cooking, no chairs to sit on.

Japan is just a dot in the map, but when you go there it's a big country. We went to some islands on a ferry boat. Japanese scenery is out of this world. The water was clear and there was a good breeze.

The streets were very narrow, but cars were small and drivers were careful. We went with a mixed group. Mama and I, Walter and Sumi and Sumi's mother, Mrs. Shizu Matsumoto of Berkeley, California, and several other Japanese families. There were about 10 Japanese out of 70 on the tour. Some good nursery friends from Baton Rouge were along, too.

Mama cried to see her home. She went to her memorial to her ancestors, and she left all her tears in Japan. She hadn't known if her home would be standing, or where her mother was buried. It had changed from rice farming to residential in her neighborhood, and her house had been modernized, but the brook was still there. My wife's auntie was still living there. She had shrunk. Japanese average 5 feet or less, so she was really small. She lived in Mama's house, but had the modern conveniences.

James Imahara receives decoration from Consul General Hiehachi Mochizuki, above; below, James and Haruka with his sister Kimi.

James Imahara with decoration medal, 1977

Land is so high and houses are small. Residents are required to have a garage if they have a car. A car in Japan is like a family treasure.

There was no trash. Everything was immaculate. The Japanese don't litter. They say it is my duty not to litter, to pick up trash and put it in its proper place. Everybody has a pride in the public places. In this country you are free to do anything, but in Japan all is clean and orderly. It is required to know manners, how to sit properly and eat properly. American money was not of much value then, though it's a little better now; but costs are higher there now, too.

Japan is a great country. I'm so proud of my ancestors' country. But I didn't have enough time to see so much. I would like to go back to Japan one more time. I am running every day to stay in shape to go back.

What I saw was very moving. Japan is my country, just as the United States of America is my country. To both I owe much, my very being. I am a part of both. I am a Japanese-American. Son of immigrants. American born of Japanese parents. That's what I am, James Imahara. And my story has much to say to the people of both countries.

I am glad to have finally told it. I hope someone will listen.

Golden Wedding Anniversary, 1977. Front row: May, James, Haruka, Irene. Second row: Walter, Flora, John, Jane, Jun, Lily, Philip.

ADDENDUM

While I was away in Chicago, my wife remained in the internment camp in Arkansas, assuming full responsibility for all the children. Here in her own words is the story of those years of my absence:

It started, for me, on December 7, 1941. Friends came to tell us of Pearl Harbor. It was a big shock, that Sunday morning. My husband spoke Japanese so everybody came to him for an explanation. He didn't know anything.

The Sacramento area was the last to be relocated. My husband helped the old Japanese-speaking *Issei*. While he was doing that and helping all the people, I had to pack our own things with my daughter May. My husband had a warden's armband, and all the Japanese people depended on him. I was pregnant with Jun, but I had to do all our packing, about 10 bags. He got everybody else off.

At first they were so strict on what could be taken; later they relaxed a little and were nicer. I brought pictures and my sewing machine—I didn't care if they killed me, I wanted to take it—and an electric clock, as well as the children's things. We left on May 30, the last family. The whole community was empty.

Why would they do this sort of thing to farmers? We were all born in the USA, had done nothing wrong.

Our friend from the produce company, the white manager, came to put us on the transports. The station was full of Japanese with bags. The American soldiers were so kind. I was not scared; they were young and taking orders, not doing bad things. Everyone was given numbers, people had tags with numbers on them, and the numbers were put on the duffel bags.

70

Photos from Mrs. Imahara's treasured album. Top left, "Ma and May." Right, Flora holding baby Jun in camp.

We took the train to the Fresno Assembly Center, a horse track where we stayed in the stables. We had American Army guards. They were sure nice, handed out candy, ice cream. My children never got hungry. I'd never say one bad thing about the American government, that's my way. My children had plenty to eat. The soldiers were just following orders. They were in uniform; that means war. There were sentry towers.

We slept on straw mattresses. The first morning I awoke and opened the window to see a soldier patrolling with a broom over his shoulder. Nobody was prepared. War is so sad for both sides.

There were communal bathrooms which scared the children, long troughs with automatic flushes of water.

All the Japanese-speaking older ones came to my husband for interpreting, and they were good to my family. The old men didn't know how to eat ice cream or boiled eggs, so they'd bring them to my children. I had 8 children, but there was enough to go around. The old *Issei* were suddenly confronted with American food and really suffered. Those old men were so good to my family, Boy, they suffered, those old ones. Chicken on Sunday was the only good meal on the army menu.

Everybody calmed down in a little while. There was no way to work out a school schedule there, everybody was there for such a short time. Everybody was so confused. The American government brought all Japanese together, some thought maybe to kill them. Everybody was scared. But I had faith in the American government.

There were 10 internment camps. We went first to Jerome in Arkansas. Some of the Japanese were wondering about mass extermination like Hitler. But it was amazing that the government had barracks and hospitals ready for us; it was fast work.

We went to Jerome in October. We were on the train five nights, four days. I had had my baby in Fresno. I would never say the American government was not good to the Japanese people. I think I know that much. The old farm people didn't know anything, just hard work.

More photos from Mrs. Imahara's pictorial record of internment camp life. Top: Mrs. Imahara. Right: Walter.

Once everybody calmed down, there were all kinds of things going on. I love sewing, so I took lessons in that. There was school for the children, and all kinds of activities. There were Japanese and American school teachers, but the management was white. My children would go to school to learn. The girls were all small, but they liked embroidery, crewel work, knitting, crocheting.

There was no radio, no TV. We were cut off from the outside, with no newspapers. We heard some things from Americans working there. I have faith in the USA; others were scared, knew about the extermination of the Jews.

Professional Japanese were paid to teach lessons. Everybody learned what they liked. There were things like flower arranging, with both fresh and crepe-paper flowers, all kinds. My children were so small, but they learned all these handicrafts.

We had a two-room area to live in. There was a cot for each of us, and an army issue mattress, not straw. We had army blankets, too. Army colors still affect me. I had brought a quilt and was glad, since it was very cold.

We could get some scrap lumber, and a friend showed me how to cut lumber, how to nail, how to make things. I became a pretty good carpenter. I made a table, bench and shelf. After the war I fussed at my husband for not making shelf.

We had a big round wood stove for heat. We were such a big family, which helped us to get more supplies. American government said children first, next pregnant women, then old people. I couldn't believe how kind the Americans were to the children and the sick.

Next we went to Rhower, Arkansas, when German prisoners were brought to Jerome.

I couldn't go out to work, I had too many children. Only professional men could leave. My husband went to Chicago to work. There was no future in the camp. The men would come back at war's end.

The atomic bomb was dropped on Hiroshima and Nagasaki. This was where my parents had been from, but they were both deceased. We heard the news probably from American offi-

Top: John at left and Walter at right in front of barracks. Right: Left to right, Walter, John, Irene and baby Jun in front.

cers. I had relatives there but most were living in the country, so I was not worried about them. It was a very sad thing. That was a beautiful city, with a big river. My relative's brother's body was under the river, never found. They just had mass graves.

They knew I had stayed in Hiroshima, so they told me the news. I was stunned more than anything, hurt. Why do people do war? They should use the mind to make peace, not dangerous weapons to hurt human beings. Still it goes on, still I hurt. "That's war," they say. I could have hit Truman for making a joke of it.

This is all my experience, not other people's. Hirohito stopped the war. After war, they made a plea for Japanese to scatter all over, not to go to one place. We were in the mess hall all together when they announced that we should relocate all over. This was what the American government told us. But the Japanese mostly went back to California.

I'm 72 now, but before I was born California had a lot of Irish. They didn't want the Japanese, who were too smart. They were scared the Japanese would take over from the Irish. They treated the Japanese almost like the Negroes were treated in the South. The Irish immigrants had power, were scared of the Japanese who had brains and worked hard. I heard that before the war for years. My husband would like to go back to California, but not me.

I want my children to stand up in this USA, not live like Papa, Mama, grandparents. I wanted to bring all these little children to New Orleans. Many people there didn't know much about the war. Some saw us as enemies, treated us like we were attackers at work and at school.

We had nobody but ourselves, but Louisiana was a good choice. I don't like the cold, and we were too poor for heat. I don't know precisely why we chose Louisiana. In camp, everybody said Louisiana people were very kind, not like Californians, but nice to everybody. In New Orleans, sure, there were some mean ones, but most were good and most were friendly.

I love Louisiana. That's my choice, my life. Everybody was asking why. I don't care about the struggle, I want my children to stand up in this world just like other nationalities. I think it all paid off.

I thought it out mostly alone. Others in the camps told about mosquitoes, alligators, swamps, snakes, jungle like Africa in Louisiana. But I knew there were lots of colleges in Louisiana, so I decided it could not be a jungle like Africa. I came for the children's sake. I want my children to stand up, get an education.

We had no money, no nothing but a hard time. In New Orleans I took in sewing. That let me take care of the children, too. I love alterations, fixing clothes. I learned drafting and fitting in camp. I have sewed all through my life. My husband's mother made clothes with no patterns, work shirts, suits; she was a very intelligent woman. I had not after all been allowed to take my original sewing machine to camp, but one American lady was so good to me, she exchanged it for a portable I could take. In New Orleans I bought a Singer.

For my children I hoped for an education. If it didn't take, the parents couldn't be blamed, but it did take for all of them.

I found out how important education is in camp. In one square mile, there were 10,000 people. In 3½ years, I watched these people, the differences among them. An education nobody can take away from you, you can support yourself. If you have no education, you are very lost, especially a woman. I did my best to give my children an education. I have no education myself, but all my children have degrees. I gave that to them. I'm not scared. They have taken over my dreams.

If you have an education and something happens, you know how to get up and go. But Japanese women were uneducated, could only be teachers, nurses, typists. Those were the only means of survival in dignity without men.

I was only nine years old when I saw my father accidentally electrocuted. I went back to Japan until I was 15. That was the Japanese way of arranging things. My mother, as the oldest son's wife, had to go back to take care of her mother-in-law. She always talked about the United States of America, said people were so kind to her there. She took the children back to Japan, but left my baby brother with an uncle here.

I didn't like Japan. Rice, I don't like it. I wanted to go back to America. My uncle said he needed a girl, so I went back to Sacramento. My Masaki uncle and aunt spoiled me. They raised Japanese vegetables, bought me silk stockings, hair combs, materials to sew with.

I went to Japanese school in Sacramento, private schools. I spoke and wrote Japanese already. My parents had come from Japan. Theirs had been an arranged marriage, and both were older. My father immigrated first, then my mother heard from a sister here and came.

My mother said good looking men had no kindness. She always advised me not to marry for looks.

When the war was over, we had hard times in Louisiana, but I did not neglect anything. It was difficult, but I was very thankful we kept the family together. You never can tell about war. I was very thankful they did not separate us or do anything to our family. We were not separated until the children married. We were very fortunate compared to Germany.

They gave us about $500 altogether at the end of the war, paying per head. The hardest times were in New Orleans. It was a struggle just to buy food, but people were so kind. They gave me beautiful clothes for my children, always helped my family. That's why I like American people. I gave three meals a day to my family, not steak, but three meals.

My children are so nice, not fussy. They went to school and learned to study, study, study. "Study" was my first word to them, "be careful" my second. I told my girls "don't fool around with men."

"Why are you so much American way," some asked me. I live in this country, I love it. I am an American. Some ask why I am so westernized. I was already an American. Everybody came from other countries to build this country. Why would anybody ask? I can't understand.

If you live in this country, why would you not be thankful for it? I appreciate everything. We were given a chance to go back to Japan at the end of the war. We all had to take a loyalty oath, answer all kinds of questions. My brother-in-law David went back to find a broken-down country, everybody starving; he came back, said there was no job, no money, no future there.

War makes your life change. That's why education is so important. It will take care of you. War can take your car, take your money, but can't take your education. You have to push, please. I had experience, myself. With an education, you're not scared, can go forth. You can support yourself, never lower yourself. Japanese women too often had to sell themselves; this was because of war and outside influence. With education, even if the worst comes, you don't have to be inferior or sell yourself. Education cost money and took courage to push for, but it is the most important thing.

After the war, my daughter May was a big help in getting loans for schooling for the others. With that many children, I had to be strong and hard-headed.

Hiroshima was strong Buddhist country, but I was always Christian. It was too hard to understand Buddhism. My mother was educated. When we came back to the U.S., my mother said, "If you die, I wait for you, whether you're Christian, Buddhist, whatever." I changed my religion in Louisiana. I was very sick with a pinched nerve, needed religion, my girls supported me when I went to a revival and joined a Christian church. My husband remains Buddhist. I needed the religion. I go to Parkview Baptist Church. The people are so nice, and it's a very beautiful church. I love to go to church. All my children are Christian, too.

I have continued to push for education with my grandchildren, too. I do this in my own way. I say I can't talk to anybody because I can't speak English right, but I get the point across in my own way. One of my grandchildren is a doctor because of me; another is going for an advanced degree because of me.

I have nine children. I raised all my children my best. My inspiration was my mother. She said to tell the truth always. This comes back. Only a mother always gives the honest truth. Among Japanese ladies there were several class distinctions.

Haruka Sunada Imahara

Ladies were very simple and modest; *geisha* girls and prostitutes were different, with different kimonos and different makeup.

I regret that I didn't get the education my parents wanted for me. I am self educated. I read a lot. But I was determined my children would get an education, no matter what. I see this world and my family, and I see a need for education, for skill.

I couldn't get my education, but I never quit reading. That's the number one form of education. I have never stopped reading, and have many Japanese American dictionaries.

We went through hard times, but I am thankful that we kept the family together and got everybody educated. I am thankful to the United States of America for this.

To order additional copies of *James Imahara—Son of Immigrants*, please send $12.50 per book, plus $1.50 postage and handling per book, to:

Son of Immigrants
℅ Imahara Nursery
12289 Florida Boulevard
Baton Rouge, Louisiana 70815